Train Like Dortmund
Play Like Dortmund

30 Exercises That Will Have Your Team Playing Like Borussia Dortmund

By Marcus DiBernardo

Table of Contents

Introduction

This book is not designed to break down Dortmund's 4-2-3-1 Formation. It is not an in depth tactical analysis of each players roles and responsibilities in the system. If you are interested in details of the 4-2-3-1 system you can pick up my book "Playing The Modern 4-2-3-1". The focus of this book is to provide you with training ground exercises that focus on the major principles and concepts that Dortmund embrace in their style of play. Each exercise directly relates to the "Training Model" that fits with Dortmund's "Game Model". The exercises focus on the four phases of the game: attacking transition, attacking organization, defensive transition and defensive organization. Dortmund is known for their quick and efficient counter attack (attacking transition), which focuses on taking advantage of the early moments of attacking transition. Once Dortmund turnover possession, they work very hard to immediately regain possession by pressing intensely (defensive transition). Playing the Dortmund style requires excellent fitness levels, strong mental commitment, high technical ability, willingness to work for the team and tactical intelligence. It is not an easy way to play but if carried out correctly, it can be extremely effective and frustrating for the opponents. There are no easy games when playing against a team like Dortmund who counter and press so well.

The sessions in the book focus on counter attacking, possession with penetrating passing, defensive pressing and developing quick technical passing ability. These exercises will have your team training like Dortmund and after time playing like

Dortmund (training model = game model). I would strongly recommend that you also read my book "Tactical Periodization: Made Simple" in order to get a greater understanding of how to organize and create a training system like the ones the top clubs in the world use.   I hope you find the exercises rewarding! As always feel free to email me with any questions or comments coachdibernardo@gmail.com

Exercise #1)
Defensive Pressing & Attacking Transition

Grid: 40x25 Yards – 4 Mannequins or Large Cones Representing Back Four
Players: 6v6
Instructions:
The red team is in possession as the blue send 3 players to press them. The blue defenders need to work as one unit to pressure and win the ball. If blue wins the ball they will play a <u>through-ball between the mannequins</u> to their 3 blue teammates in the other half of the grid (this would be the stage of attacking transition). The blue players would all run into the grid making the game 3 red versus 6 blue - the 3 red players will try to press and win the ball. The game continues in this fashion going back and forth at a very high tempo. The emphasis is on defensive pressing, attacking transition (looking to play forward to the opposite grid as soon as the ball is won) and moving the ball quickly to relieve pressure from the pressing. All these points of emphasis in the exercise are very important for the way Dortmund play.

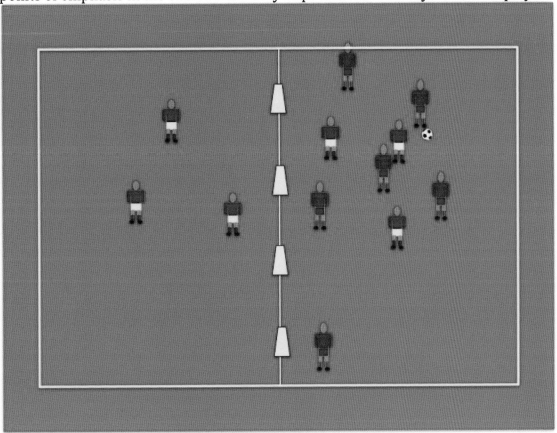

Exercise #2
Defensive Pressing & Attacking Transition To Small Goals

Grid: 40x25 Yards – 6 Small Sided Goals
Players: 6v6
Instructions:
This exercise is a progression of exercise #1 (you can keep mannequins or not) with 3 small-sided goals on each end line. The game is played exactly the same as exercise #1. The change comes when the defense wins the ball and plays the ball back into their 3 teammates (they will run to join their teammates and the opponents will send 3 players to press). If the new team in possession can make 3 passes, they can score on any of the 3 small goals in their grid for a point. The idea is for the new team in possession to play very quickly before the 3 pressuring defenders can stop them. If the team scores they will keep the ball and the 3 defenders will continue to press until they win the ball and go into attacking transition. There are all types of variations that can be made with this exercise.
Variations: Change the number of passes to be completed before scoring, add a neutral player making it 7v3 in possession, create a touch restriction or send 4 players instead of 3.

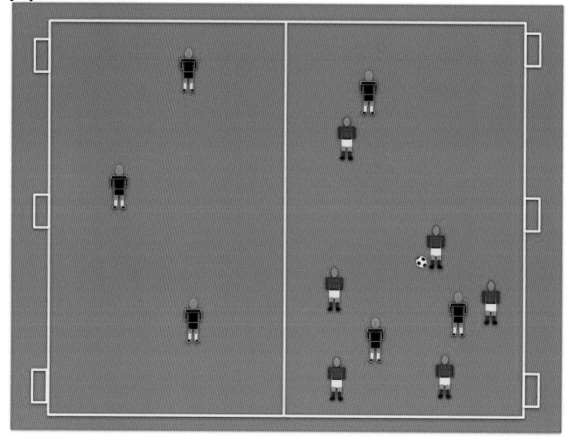

Exercise #3
Defensive Pressing & Attacking Transition To Large Goals

Grid: 40x25 Yards – 2 Regular Goals
Players: 6v6 + Keepers
Instructions:
This exercise is similar to #1 & #2. When the defensive player wins the ball and plays the ball back to his teammates in the opposite grid, they must make 3 passes before scoring on the keeper in that half. The opponents are sending 3 defenders to try and stop the 3 passes and cut out any shot on goal. 1 point is awarded for each goal that is scored. If the attacking team misses the shot the coach will play a new ball into the opposite grid (transition). If the keeper saves the shot, the keeper will throw the ball to the opposite grid, starting attacking transition. **Variations:** send 4 players instead of 3 for defensive pressing, change pass requirements before scoring on goal (less to create more scoring chance and faster transition or more passes to allow the defense to recover), add a neutral player who floats with whatever team is in possession, have a time limit to get a shot off (example: 8 seconds or less).

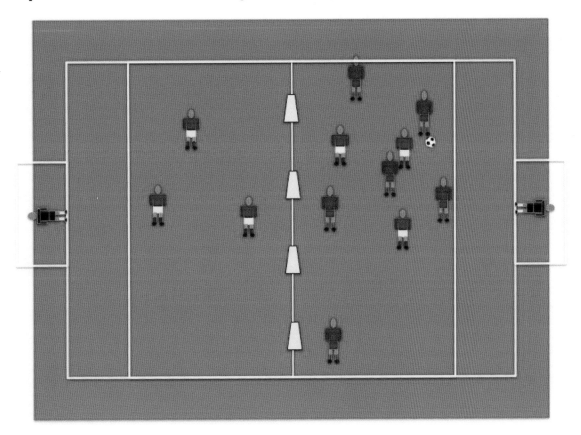

Exercise #4
Defensive Pressing Into Attacking Transition

Grid: 45x20 Yards – 2 Regular Goals
Players: 4v4 + 4 Neutral Players
Instructions:
This is another excellent exercise that starts with pressing and transfers into attacking transition. These high-pressure and high intensity exercises that focus on transition are very important in the Dortmund style of play. The blue team is in possession and can use any of the 3 outside red players to keep possession. If the orange/black team intercept the ball they immediately look to play forward into the next grid to the far red outside neutral player – when this happens all the players on both teams sprint and transition into the far grid. The two outside red sideline players will also shift down to make it 4+3 in possession in the new grid. I like this exercise because it makes players press with commitment and as soon as they regain the ball, their first thought is attacking transition forward to the far outside neutral red player. The exercise mimics the demands of the real game and enforces the speed of attacking transition and the importance of coordinated pressing.

Exercise #5
Possession With Penetrating Forward Running & Passing

Grid: 40 x 30 yards
Players: 18
Instructions:

In order to score a point the end zone player must switch places with a wide player. The wide player times his run to receive the ball on the run into the end zone. The opposing teams players in the end zone and wide zones are not allowed to defend. The idea is create coordinated timed forward runs that penetrate the end zone. In this example the blue team is set up in Dortmund's 4-2-3-1 (with out the center backs) and they have two #9's – one in each end zone. The #7 and #11 are the wide players looking to cut through the field on diagonal runs switching places with the #9 and scoring. The example below shows the blue team combining in midfield and releasing the penetrating pass to the #7 cutting into the end zone as the #9 takes #7's place out wide. The teams in the middle can play an outside teammate in the wide or end zone at any time but it will not be a point. The only way to score is the penetrating timed runs into the end zone with wide players switching places with the #9's. The team defending will focus on pressing, while the team in possession will look to penetrate quickly in attack. The Dortmund theme of fast attacking transition and defensive pressing is again emphasized in this training exercise. In order to have players work at maximum intensity it is important to have them play 2-3 minutes and than rest 1 minute. Do not let the exercise go for 35 minutes straight without rest, because the maximum effort will not last and the training will not be game realistic.

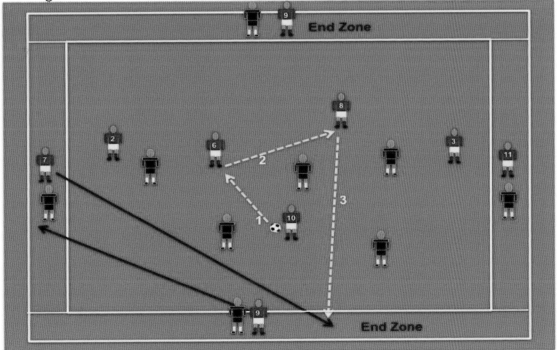

Addition of a Neutral Player:
This is the same exercise only with the addition of a neutral player to help move the ball quicker and create more scoring chances. The defensive team will now have to be smarter in their pressing.

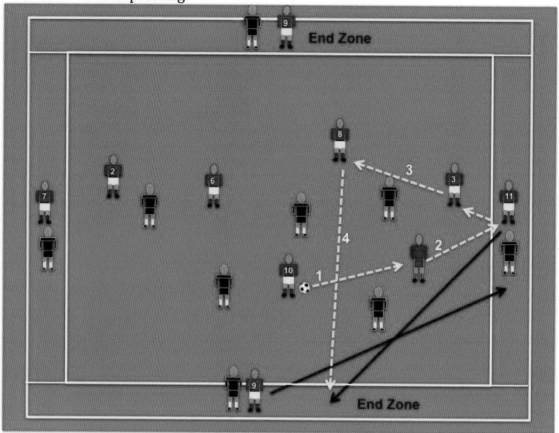

Exercise #6
Position Specific Timed Finishing In The 4-2-3-1 Formation

Grid: 35 x 30 yards
Players: 9 field players, 1 keeper and 1 target player
Instructions:
The blue team is set-up in the 4-2-3-1 (without the back four). They are given 2 minutes to score as many goals against the defensive back three & keeper. If the keeper or the defenders win the ball they must get it to the target player up top as quick as possible. If the blue team losses possession they will immediately press to win it back from the defenders and try to score. Once the ball is out of bounce or the target has received the ball the play is over. The coach will start a new ball right away with the attacking team. The attacking team plays with the urgency to score as quick as possible and as much as possible in the 2-minute time frame. This exercise allows the attacking team to get many attacking repetitions in the 4-2-3-1 formation. It also goes from attack to defending transition and even back to attacking transition if the ball is lost and won again. As with all the exercises it is important the players use maximum effort at game speed. Allow a rest period of 60-90 seconds between each 2-minute effort. **Variations:** add a defender, add wingbacks for the attacking team, must get a shot off in 8 or less seconds.

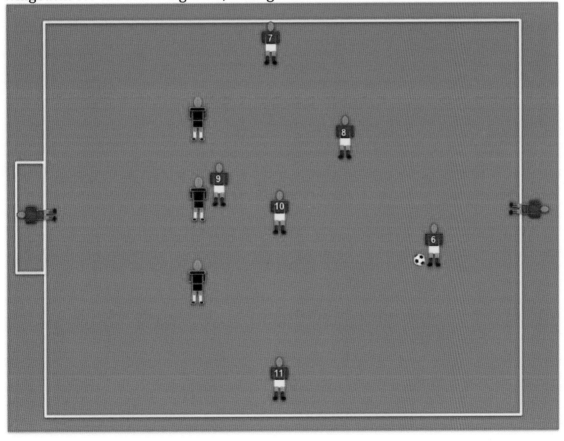

Exercise #7
Counter Attacking At Speed

Grid: 35 x 30 yards
Players: 10 field players & 2 keepers
Instructions:
This 3v2 counter attacking exercise focuses on intercepting the ball and immediately going into attacking transition- 3v2 to goal. The exercise starts with the black/orange team playing the ball towards the mannequin as the 3rd blue player steps in front and intercepts the ball. The blue team then goes at speed towards goal trying to score. If the black/orange team intercepts the ball or the keeper makes the save – they will go 2v1 the other direction against the blue team. The player who gave away the ball or shot the ball will be the 1 defender. The exercise is continuous with the next group ready come on. Dortmund look to counter attack immediately off intercepted passes. This exercise simulates the interception and then the counter attack is live. **Variations:** 5 attackers and 3 defenders, 2 touch restriction, 1 touch finish, score within 7 seconds.

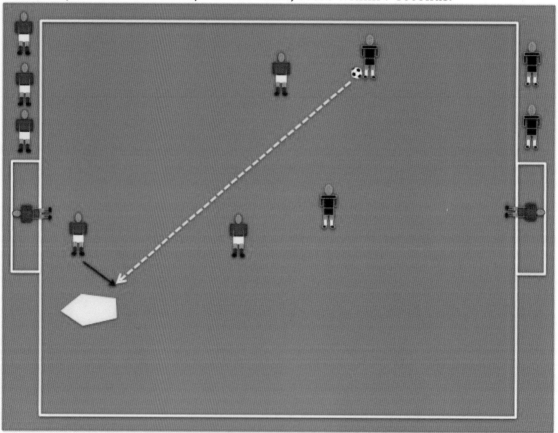

Exercise #8
Counter Attacking At Speed 5v3 Continuous

Grid: 40 x 30
Players: 11 field players & 2 keepers
Instructions:
This fast paced counter attacking game requires quick transition and decision-making. The 2 players in white are always on the team attacking in possession – making it a 5v3 to goal. The attacking team has 10 seconds or less to score or else the ball is turned over. Below, the blue team and 2 white players attack the orange/black team and try to score. If the orange/black team intercept the ball they will attack quickly the far goal against the purple team (who comes running on to defend). The blue team will now be at the other end waiting to come back on. If the purple win the ball they will attack the blue team. If orange/black score on the purple they will keep the ball and attack the other direction on the blue team. The exercise is continuous and at a fast pace. The exercise includes defending and attacking transition with the emphasis on speed of play and countering. Becoming proficient in attack requires training and this exercise is another useful exercise in building a teams ability to counter. The drill fits the Dortmund philosophy of play with fast paced attacking transition.. **Variations:** adjust time limits to score, add a 4th player, add touch restrictions.

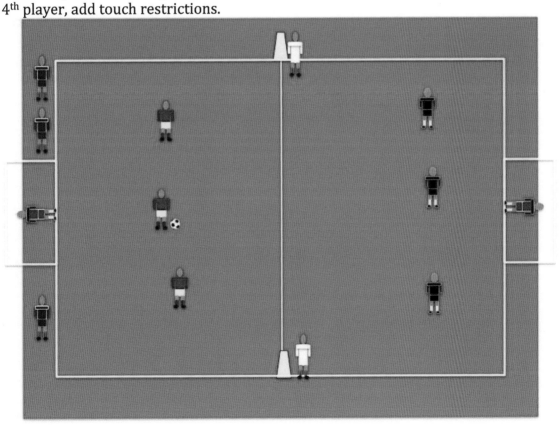

Exercise #9
4-2-3-1 Wide Counter Attacking 10v10

Grid: Penalty Box - Penalty Box
Instructions & Key Points:
9v9 + Keepers: 4 neutral corner players. Teams look to counter & play the ball wide & deep to a neutral "yellow" corner player. The corner player will look to play in an early cross to players who are making runs into the box. Variation: Allow the neutral corner player to dribble in towards the goal looking to pass to an attacking player running into the box. This a very realistic game exercise in relation to the way Dortmund play. The counter attack is the priority and when the ball is lost pressing is carried out. The 4-2-3-1 formation is used (missing 1 CB). **Key Points:** have attacking players time their runs into the box, think of the cross as a pass to player into the box, the shot is the final pass placed into the net, make sure attackers vary their runs.

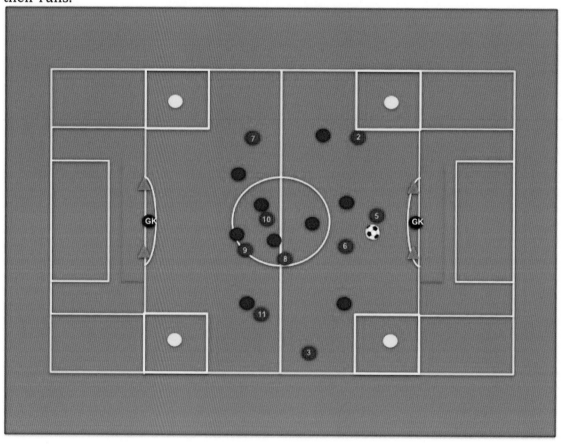

Exercise #10
4-2-3-1 Wide Counter Attacking 11v11

Grid: ¾ Field
Instructions & Key Points:
The red attacking team must pass to a yellow corner neutral player when attacking. Red attacking players will then attack the three marked boxes in the box. The Red players can only score from runs into one of the three boxes. The Blue team will attack the red teams goal when they gain possession. The red team will carry out pressing when they lose possession. **Key Points:** have attacking players time their runs into the box, think of the cross as a pass to player into the box, the shot is the final pass placed into the net, make sure attackers vary their runs.

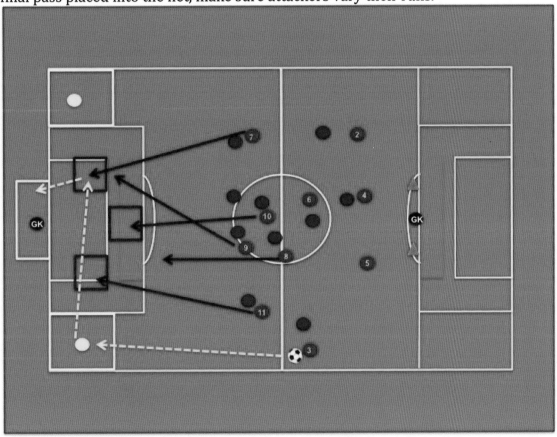

Exercise #11
4-2-3-1 Winger/Wingback Different Channels Conditioned Game

Grid: Penalty Box – Penalty Box
Instructions & Key Points:
10v10 + Keepers – There are four outside channels located out wide. The wingback and winger are not allowed to stand in the same channel when in possession. The wingback will occupy one channel and the winger the other. In the diagram below, the red wingback #2 occupies the inner channel and the red winger #7 occupies the wider channel, the same as the #3 & #11. The positioning and movement between the wingback and winger must be understood by both players in order for the team use the width effectively in attack. This exercise forces players to position themselves correctly in a game realistic situation. Teams like Dortmund that play the 4-2-3-1 must have very good coordination between the wingback and winger. When one cuts in the other makes the space out wide. **Key Points:** if the winger cuts inside the wingback must get forward to offer attacking width in the final 1/3, when the ball is lost both players can get compact or if needed immediately press, when the ball is won one of the two players must fill the channel wide.

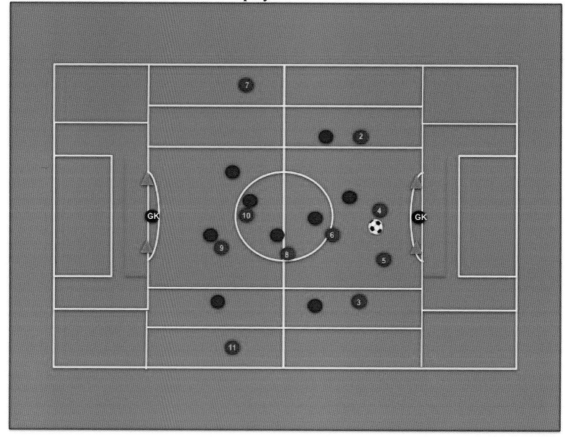

Exercise #12
Movement & Possession in 4-2-3-1 Formation

Grid: 40 x 30 yards
Players: 14 field players
Instructions:
This exercise teaches movement in the 4-2-3-1 formation. The blue team is set-up in the 4-2-3-1 without the CB's. The blue team's objective is to move the ball will using coordinated timed movement between the players. In the below example, notice the wingers #11 & #7 both cut inside leaving their marked square to form a triangle between the 7,11,9 & 10. After the players located in a side box make their movement outside the box they must eventually return inside the box again. If the orange/black team intercepts the ball the blue players not in the boxes must press them right away to win the ball back. This exercise is good for the players understanding of team shape and movement in the 4-2-3-1 formation.

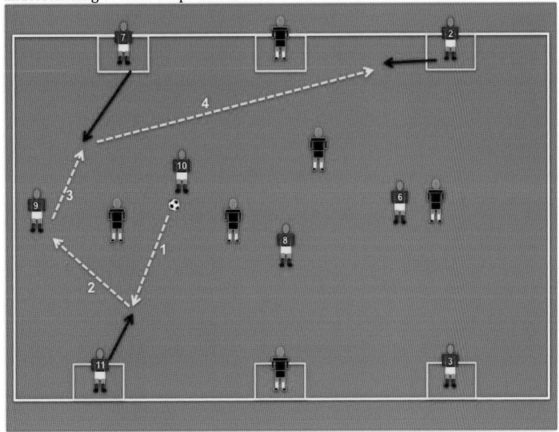

Exercise #13
Isolating The Midfield In The 4-2-3-1 Formation

Grid: 20 x 20 yards
Players: 10 field players
Instructions:
This exercise works on the midfield unit and one CB. The blue team works the ball in possession 1-2 touch. If the orange/black wins the ball they attempt to keep the possession and can use their one outside player. This exercise is made to keep the ball circulating at a rapid pace in the specific 4-2-3-1 formation. Rapid ball circulation is something Dortmund can do very well in the 4-2-3-1 formation. The quick movement of the ball is essential at high levels of play.

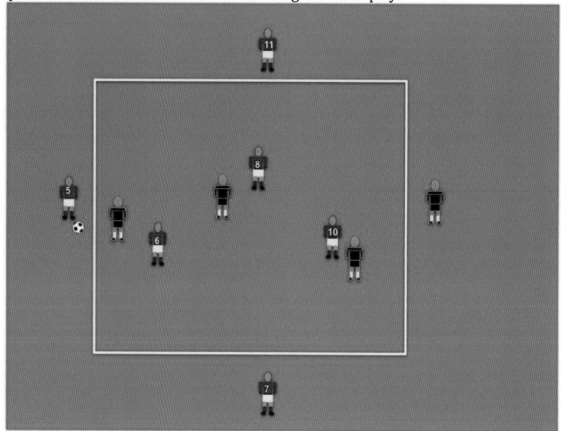

Variation:
Grid: 20 x 20 yard square and a 35x25 yard space in front of the square
Players: 11 field players + keeper
Instructions:
This exercise just builds on the previous and adds a striker #9 with a defender in the attacking 1/3. A minimum of 4 passes is required before playing forward into the #9. The wingers #7, #11 and #10 can release into the attack as well. The orange/black team can release 2 defenders once the ball is passed out of the square into the forward (4v3 for blue on attack). This exercise provides many attacking reps in the 4-2-3-1 formation. **Variations:** feel free to mix the numbers and touch restrictions and even set a time limit to score once the ball is passed out of the square.

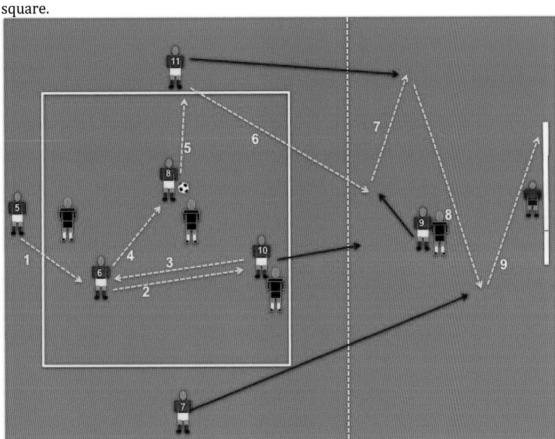

Exercise #14
Counter Attacking In The 4-2-3-1 Formation

Grid: 15 x 15 yard small box for 4v4 + attacking 1/3 of field
Players: 16 field players + keeper
Instructions:
The blue team starts with the ball inside the 15x15 yard small box. When the orange/black team intercepts the ball they release 3 players to make a 6v4 counter attack. If the black/orange team wins the ball they can also play it back to the player outside the box & behind to start the counter. **Variations**: This is a basic set-up for the counter attack. You can adjust the numbers in the counter attack and in defense for 4v1, 4v2, 4v3, 4v4, 5v4, 6v4 and even have blue players from the box recover to defend. The focus of the exercise is to win the ball from the blue team and immediately go into attacking transition at speed, finishing with a shot on goal. Not all counters start by going forward which is why 1 orange/black player is positioned behind the box – some counters have to start with a pass back then square ball and then forward. This exercise fits perfectly into the Dortmund style – work hard to win the ball and transition into a fast counter. Defensive transition to attacking transition.

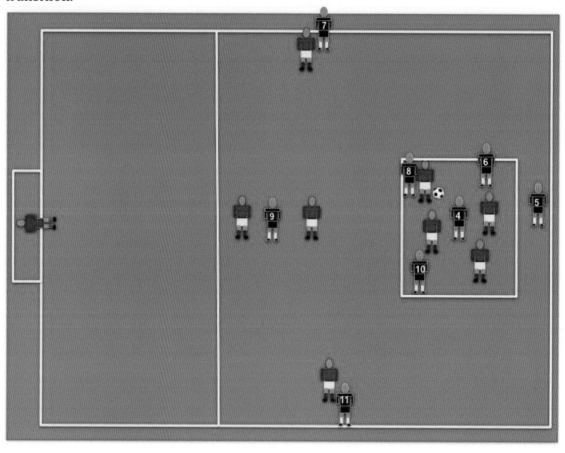

Exercise #15
Possession To Penetrate

Grid: 60x35 yards – split into 3 zones of 15/30/15 yards
Players: 17 field players
Instructions:
The play starts in the middle zone with 4v4+1 Neutral (on team with the ball). The team in possession must complete 4 passes before playing into their forward pair. When the forward 2 players receive the ball, 1 player from the middle zone can join them making it a 3v2 in the final attacking zone. In order to score the team of 3 (2 forwards & 1 player from middle) must play a penetrating ball through the mannequins (representing the back 4) to a player running in behind into the end zone. The player must stop the ball in the end zone for a point. Players can't stand in the end zone and wait for the penetrating pass, they must time their run to break into the zone to stop the pass for a point – the 4 mannequins are the offsides line as well.

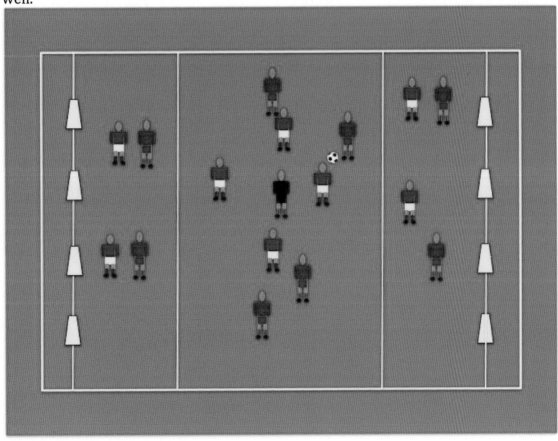

Exercise #16
Team Possession To Penetrate

Grid: 60x35 yards
Players: 18 field players
Instructions:
The game is 6v6 with 6 outside neutrals who are limited to 1-touch on the outside. In order to score a penetrating pass must be made between the mannequins (representing the back 4) to a teammate running in and behind that stops the ball in the end zone. Either team can use the outside neutral players. This is a fast paced game with the intent of probing and looking for those penetrating runs and balls to open up the back four. The game is excellent for forward penetrating passing and running, it is very useful in a counter attacking system or a possession system.

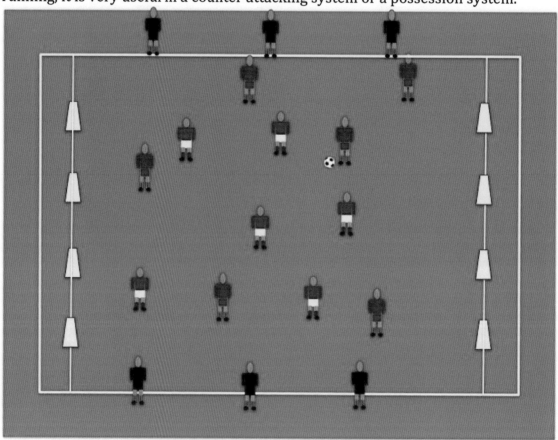

Exercise #17
Team Possession To Penetrate on Goal

Grid: 60x35 yards – Divided into 3 zones of 20/20/20 yards
Players: 14 field players + 2 keepers
Instructions:
This exercise focuses on attacking quickly and getting numbers forward. The ball starts in the middle grid as the team tries to play a ball into their forwards – 1 midfield player can join the forwards in attack making it a 3v2. Start the game with 3 passes in the middle before playing into the forward pair. **Variation:** allow 2 midfields to join the attack for a 4v2, allow 2 midfielders to attack and 1 midfielder to go back on defense for a 4v3, adjust the number of passes required before playing into the forwards. Feel free to work on many variations in this exercise. This type of drill re-enforces penetrating balls, forward thinking, movements of the attacking pair, midfield forward running and finishing.

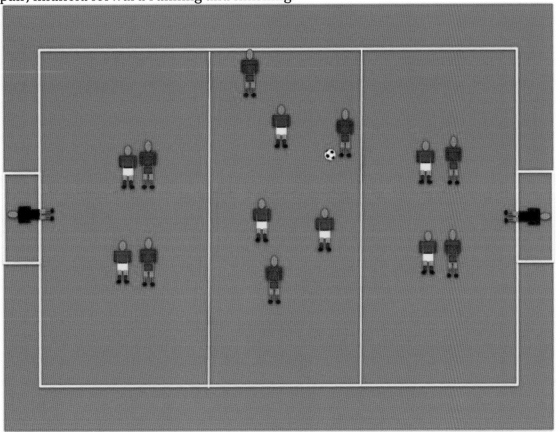

Exercise #18
Quick Possession, Switching The Field & Counter Attacking

Grid: 75 x 60 yards
Players: 19 field players + 1 keeper
Instructions:
The red team is trying to score on the goal with the keeper. The blue team scores by stopping the ball in the far end zone opposite the goal. They must play a pass that travels into the end zone as one of the players must run into the zone and stop the ball for a point. Players are not allowed to stand in the end zone and wait for a pass. The field is also divided into 4 sections (squares). Teams are allowed to make 2 passes in a square and then the 3rd pass must be played into another square or section of the field. Having this condition forces play to speed up and players to increase their vision. The team scoring on the end zone should look for fast transitions into attack because they have the entire end zone to score on (they won't need to keep possession endlessly because the area to score on is so large).

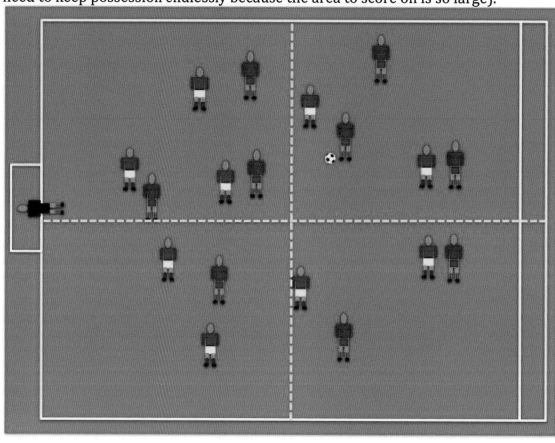

Functional Technical Training Needed To Play Like Dortmund

I included this next section on passing and receiving because modern soccer demands that teams move the ball extremely fast. In order to be successful in possession, counter attacking and overcoming the intense pressing of today's game; teams must be technical, intelligent and move the ball quick. Dortmund prides them selves on the speed at which they execute their "attacking transition" phase of the game. They move the ball so efficiently, fast and direct on the counter attack; they make it very difficult for the opponent to get numbers back to defend. The opponent is often stuck in defensive transition without enough time to shift into defensive organization (they can get numbers back fast enough). Transition in today's game is so quick, teams must be trained to react immediately whenever the ball is won or lost (most important time of the game). Fast & effective attacking transition requires tactical intelligence, excellent technique, some physically gifted players and speed of thought. The "German Football Federation" came out last year with a statement saying, they wanted their midfield players to release the ball in 9/10th of a second or less in order to compete in todays fast paced game. "Pinging" the ball around with a purpose in less than 9/10th of second per/player sounds nice, but it requires years of practice. Players must be trained to scan the field, look over their shoulder before receiving the ball, receive the ball away from pressure to their back foot into depth, receive the ball on the ½ turn looking forward if possible (so you can play forward quickly), understand when to play first time balls to a player in a better position, have knowledge & understanding of angles, movement, timing and body positions when receiving the ball. These are skills that many coaches and players overlook, but eventually without these skills the player and team will fall behind in their development and progress. Take the example of the "Croatia National Soccer Federation" compared to the "United States Soccer Federation". The Croatia National Soccer Team has never beaten the US U14 National Team. Croatia is a very well coached technical soccer country that is a fraction of the size of the United States (I mean tiny). The United States teams at the U14 level are athletic, fast and strong. These physical characteristics propel the United States forward at the younger levels. However, the US National Team U18 all the way to the full Senior Men's National Team has never beaten Croatia! Why is this? The answer to me is simple. The US soccer development system is simply not good enough. Look at Dortmund, they are both physically imposing and possess enormous technical ability and soccer intelligence. The following exercises are similar to what Croatia uses in their developmental program. In order to play like Dortmund, make sure you include game realistic technical exercises like the ones in this section, which fit into the Dortmund training and game model.

The receiving player has a man on his back and takes a flat angle to receive the ball. His only real option is 1-touch back. This is a good option and you see it all the time in games. However, the reality is that the player has limited vision and opportunities to pass the ball into depth (penetrating balls). Could the player have found space? Could the player have run away from pressure to receive the ball?

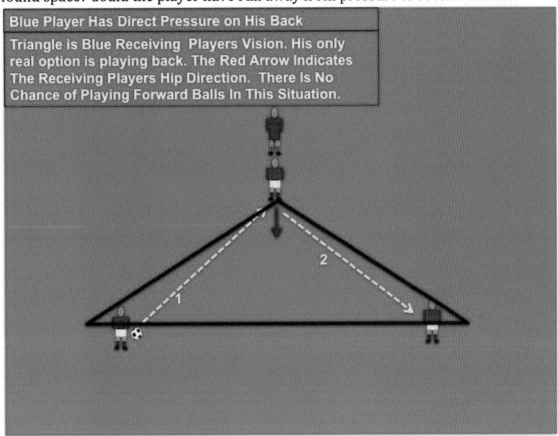

Blue Player Has Direct Pressure on His Back

Triangle is Blue Receiving Players Vision. His only real option is playing back. The Red Arrow Indicates The Receiving Players Hip Direction. There Is No Chance of Playing Forward Balls In This Situation.

In this example the player is receiving the ball with his hips facing the passing player. This limits vision and opportunities to play to depth. This position takes to much time to turn up field and it allows the defense to settle in behind the ball. It also restricts the player's options because his vision is restricted by his hip position.

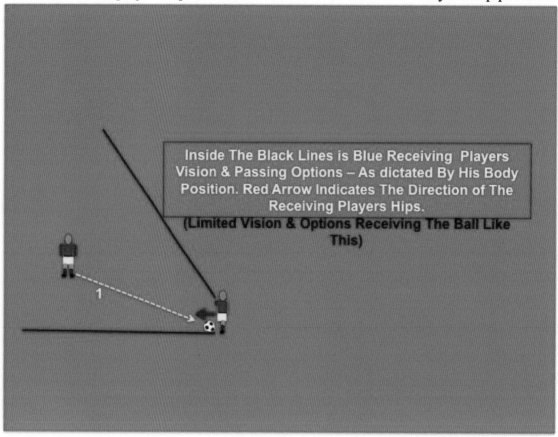

Inside The Black Lines is Blue Receiving Players Vision & Passing Options – As dictated By His Body Position. Red Arrow Indicates The Direction of The Receiving Players Hips.
(Limited Vision & Options Receiving The Ball Like This)

The player now is opening his hips slightly more to receive the pass and as a result has increased forward vision. This is still not ideal but is better than the previous example. The opportunity to play some forward balls and see the field is slightly improved.

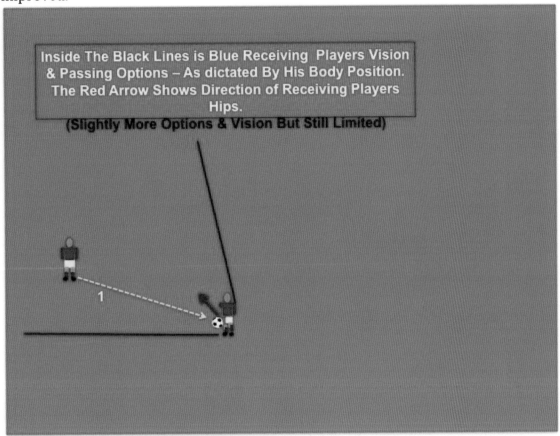

Inside The Black Lines is Blue Receiving Players Vision & Passing Options – As dictated By His Body Position. The Red Arrow Shows Direction of Receiving Players Hips.
(Slightly More Options & Vision But Still Limited)

This example shows the player with his hips open receiving the ball to his back foot. Look at the vision he has and look at the amount of forward options he can see. Playing the ball to depth now will be simple (meaning playing forward balls penetrating the defensive line). You should be able to see that the proper use of technique will bring about more vision and options on the ball – the cognitive processes involved in decision making and picking out the most effective passes intertwine with the use of intelligent well executed technique.

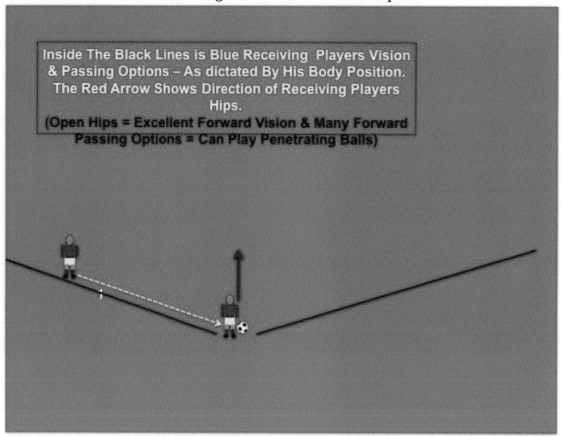

Here we see the player relieving pressure with a smart little run that results in receiving the ball on the ½ turn. Look at the vision and forward passing opportunities created by this intelligent movement of the receiving player. Intelligent runs, movement, angles, timing, speed and technique allow players to see more and have more options on the ball. The cognitive processing of higher-level players is different because they set the game up differently and put themselves in different situations than lower level players. Higher level-players can think faster and make quicker decisions – past experiences play a large part as well. However, all the past experiences in the world with improper technique and below average coaching will not help a player's development.

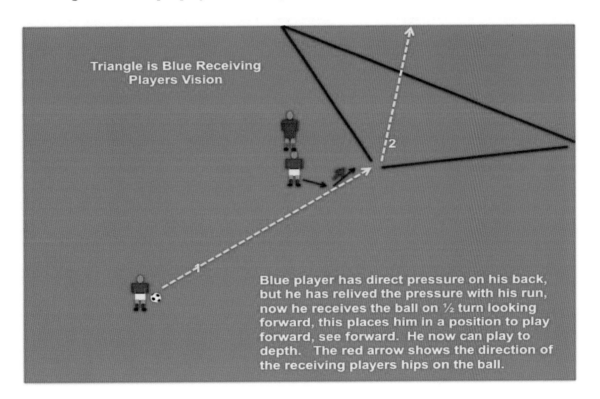

Triangle is Blue Receiving
Players Vision

Blue player has direct pressure on his back, but he has relived the pressure with his run, now he receives the ball on ½ turn looking forward, this places him in a position to play forward, see forward. He now can play to depth.   The red arrow shows the direction of the receiving players hips on the ball.

Here is a simple vision exercise that has three progressions of overloads. The player in the middle receives the ball ½ turned for his control touch and must identify the colors that are held up – you can start with identifying just 1 color in the upper corner and eventually work towards scanning for all four colors in the corners. This is a great drill for scanning, vision and technical ½ turn receiving of the ball for forward passing and vision. You may modify this drill any way you wish – the important thing is the idea. In order to shift into effective transition players must be able to receive the ball in positions they can play forward from.

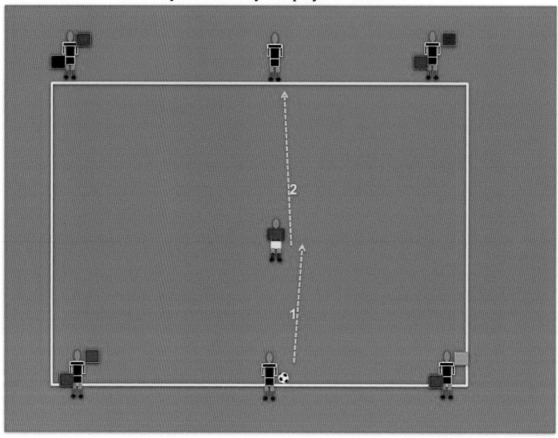

Progression/Overload: Side players are added with color cards to be identified.

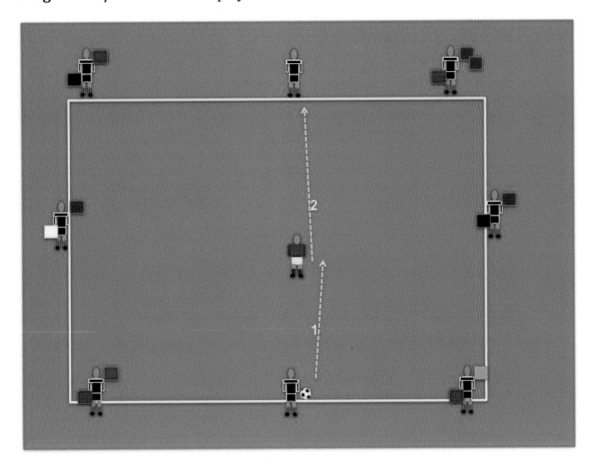

Progression/Overload: Now even the passers have cards to identify. If the player can identify all 8 cards they have scanned the entire 360 degrees! There are many ways to set-up these types of exercises.

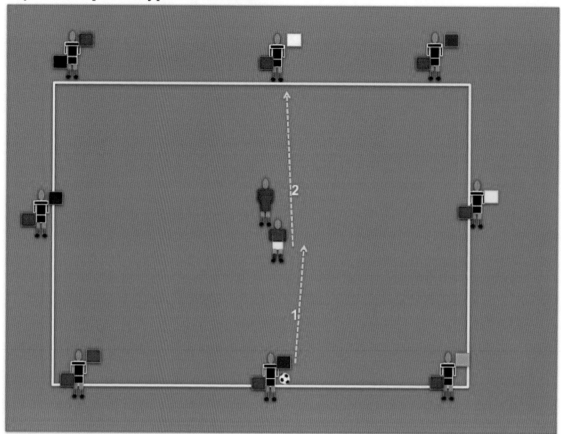

PASSING EXERCISES: CUEING, GRIDDING & VISUALIZATION

This exercise is to get players use to receiving and the ball on the back foot and playing to the back foot very quickly in 2-touches with speed and precision. High level soccer demands these skills.

Cueing Passing: Diamond

The cones serve as visual external spatial cues. This pattern is in the form of a diamond. Player's work from inside to outside & can also work outside to inside (concentric and eccentric movement). The pattern requires coordinated movement between players that simulates actual game movement. Back foot 2-touch inside of foot passing

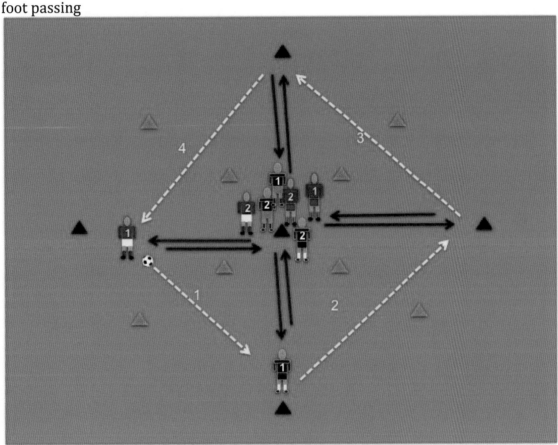

Cueing Passing: Diamond

This diamond passing exercise uses 4 players instead of 8. The players are now moving from outside to inside. Back foot passing – 2-touch inside of foot. 1 ball. However many variations can be made with these types of passing exercises. Examples: vary the runs to add angles, play 1-touch to back foot, play 2-touch left foot control right foot pass, play right foot control and right foot pass, play ball in air allowing 1 bounce before the next player who touches it once and than bounce and then 2nd touch ball is sent to the next player. The number of variations on most these drills is unlimited. However, keep the tempo and passing realistic to the game.

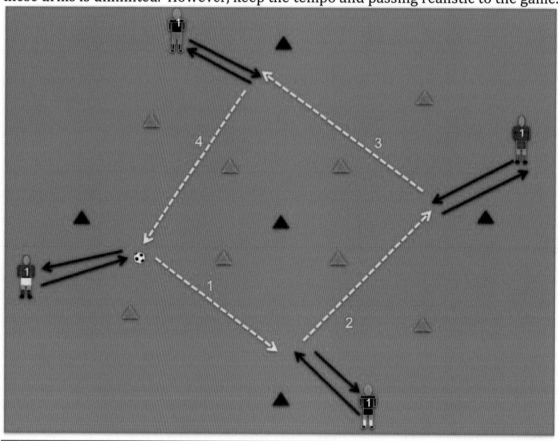

Cueing Passing: Diamond

This Pattern uses 2 balls with same principles as the previous passing exercises. The pattern can be done from inside to outside or outside to inside. The main difference is the increased synchronization and rhythm that is required between all the groups to keep both balls moving together with proper spacing. A nice variation is to have players play a 3-touch sequence with their partner before moving the ball to the next group. This simple variation require the first touch to be back the players partner who is in support, the partner 1-touches the ball back and the last pass is 1-touch to the next group. The partners would simply change roles for the next rotation.

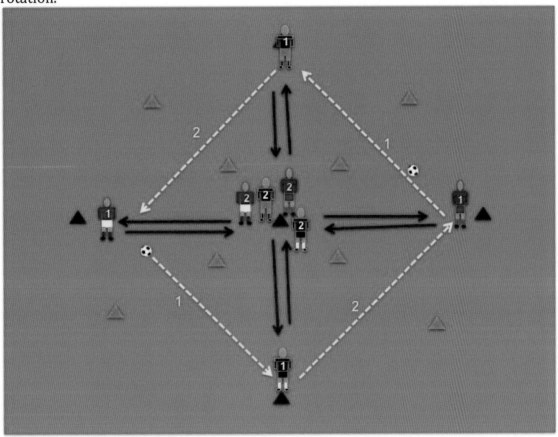

This simple exercise teaches players who have pressure from behind to pass the ball backwards to a player who is in a better position. At Barcelona they teach players to respect their teammates who are in a better position then them by passing the ball first time. This is not a difficult drill but it is important for decision-making.

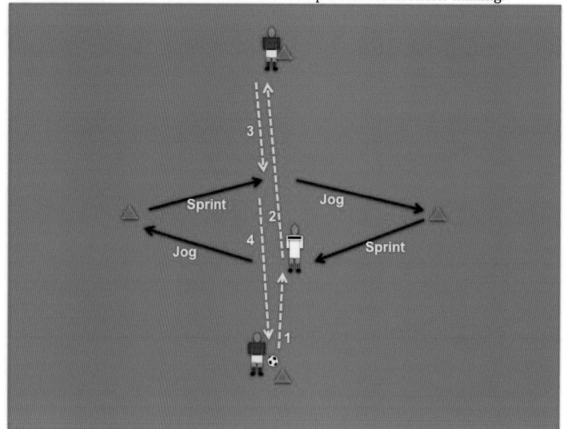

In this exercise the player pulls off of the cone (cone simulates the defender) receives the ball on the ½ turn into depth on the back foot and passes to the player on the far side. The middle player than moves to the other side of the center cone and pulls off the cone in the opposite direction –receiving the ball on the ½ turn into depth on the back foot (using the opposite foot). Always practice using both feet.

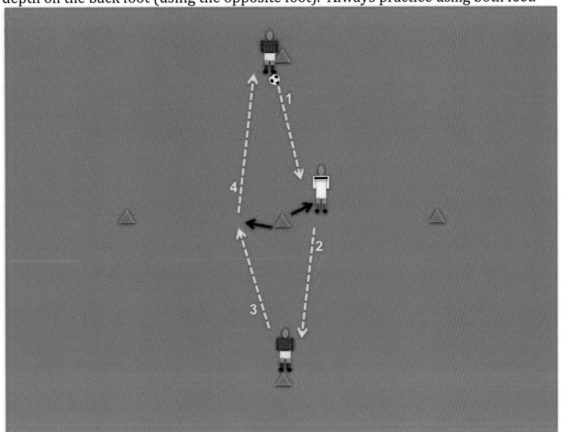

This exercise has two zones marked. A small zone marked by the red cones and the larger zone marked by the black cones. The white player in the middle works on receiving the ball side-on, turning in 1-touch and passing on the 2nd touch to the opposite side server. The white player creates space, turns and passes all in the small red zone (creates space by moving quick couple feet). Working in tight spaces with quality fast execution is very important because in a real game time and space can close in an instant.

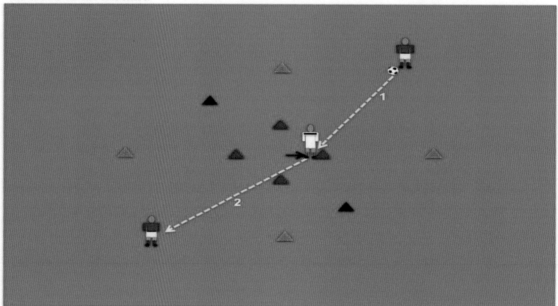

The next variation is 1-touch back from red zone, check into zone 2 (between red and black cones) and turn and play to other side in 2-touches. The turning player is learning about angles, movement, timing and spacing using the zones.

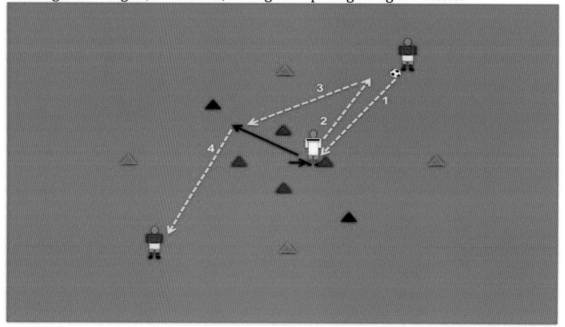

This variation requires zone#1 turn and pass to either side player in 2-touches total. Playing into the side players back foot. The pass into the side players back foot must be accurate and firm. These skills seem simple but they are very important and not so easy to be consistently with. Practice these types of skills on a daily basis.

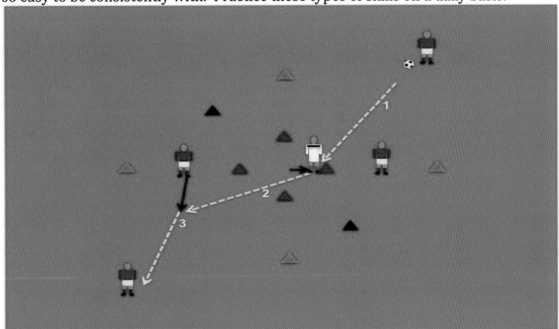

Variation: The addition of a passive defender is now added and the turn and pass is executed in zone#2. Same 2-touches for the turn + pass.

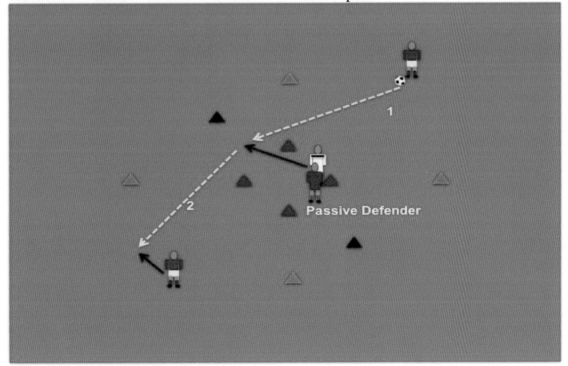

This color-coded exercise is intended to vary the angles and directions the player receives the ball at, while requiring them to play quick and efficiently. It is important the players minimize their steps and foot movement when receiving and passing the ball, receive the ball in 1-touch with hips open and hit the pass in a compact style with short follow through motion to improve speed, fast & tight movements only. The coach will yell out a new color and the players will start from that color cone to move and receive the ball. When the pass is in flight the player will begin to move from the cone in coordination with the pass (it could be backwards, forwards, from the left or right). The idea is accurate quick passing in the most efficient way possible.

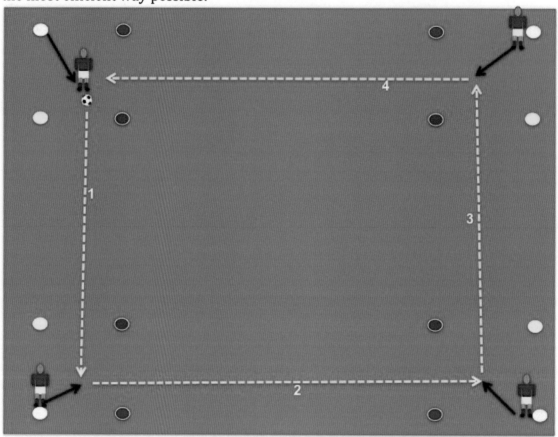

This next variation now has the player following his pass into the next box. The same principles apply as the previous exercise. The coach will yell out the color to start from. The only difference is movement is now added by running forward after the pass.

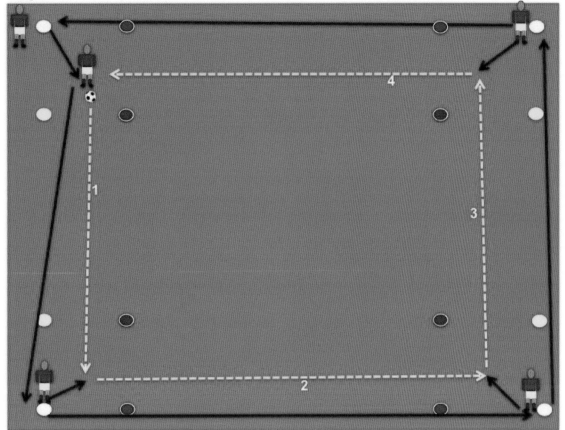

This set-up is similar to the last two exercises but this exercise is in the shape of a diamond. The two middle players need to turn 1-touch and play the pass on their 2nd touch forward. The emphasis is on fast execution of passing, receiving into depth and minimizing time on the ball.

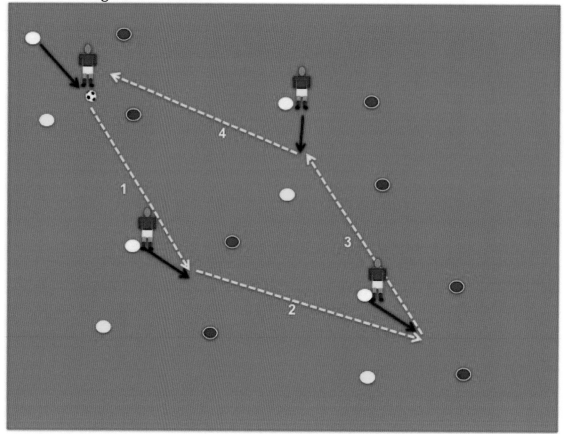

This exercise is a variation of the last exercise, but now the players follow their passes to the next square. The coach will call out the color the players will start from.

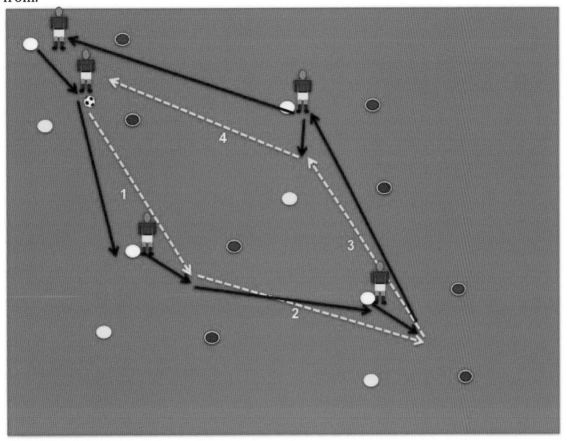

Printed in Great Britain
by Amazon.co.uk, Ltd.,
Marston Gate.